Primary Sources of Colonial America

Slavery in Colonial America

Alison Morretta

Cavendish Square

New York

Library of Congress Cataloging-in-Publication Data

Names: Morretta, Alison, author.
Title: Slavery in colonial America / Alison Morretta.
Description: New York : Cavendish Square Publishing, 2018. | Series: Primary sources of colonial America | Includes bibliographical references and index.
Identifiers: LCCN 2017020657 (print) | LCCN 2017021699 (ebook) | ISBN 9781502631435 (E-book) | ISBN 9781502631428 (library bound) | ISBN 9781502634603 (pbk.)
Subjects: LCSH: Slavery--United States--History--17th century--Juvenile literature. | Slavery--United States--History--18th century--Juvenile literature. | African Americans--Social conditions--17th century--Juvenile literature. | African Americans--Social conditions--18th century--Juvenile literature.
Classification: LCC E446 (ebook) | LCC E446 .M73 2018 (print) | DDC 306.3/62097309032--dc23
LC record available at https://lccn.loc.gov/2017020657

Editorial Director: David McNamara
Editor: Fletcher Doyle
Copy Editor: Rebecca Rohan
Associate Art Director: Amy Greenan
Designer: Lindsey Auten
Production Coordinator: Karol Szymczuk
Photo Research: J8 Media

The photographs in this book are used by permission and through the courtesy of: Photos credits: Cover http://www.nycreligion.info/Wikimedia Commons/File:First Slave Auction 1655 Howard Pyle.jpg/CC PD; p. 5 http://www.learnnc.org/Wikimedia Commons/File:1670 virginia tobacco slaves.jpg/CC PD; p. 6, 44 North Wind Picture Archives/Alamy Stock Photo; p. 8, 11 Hulton Archive/Getty Images; p. 13, 48 Everett Historical/Shutterstock.com; p. 15 PresidentistVB (Dr. Matt Hogendobler)/Wikimedia Commons/File:Anthony Johnson MARKE 600.png/CC SA-BY 3.0; p. 17 Smith Collection/Gado/Archive Photos/Getty Images; p. 19 Lanmas/Alamy Stock Photo; p. 23 DEA/G. Dagli Orti/De Agostini Picture Library/Getty Images; p. 24 Schomburg Center for Research in Black Culture, Manuscripts, Archives and Rare Books Division/The New York Public Library; p. 26 Peter Newark American Pictures/Bridgeman Images; p. 32 North Wind Picture Archives; p. 34-35 Waters_Justin/Wikimedia Commons/File:Fort Mose Panorama.jpg/CC BY-SA 4.0; p. 40 PHAS/Universal Images Group/Getty Images; p. 46 Susan Law Cain/Shutterstock.com; p. 51 Charles Phelps Cushing/ClassicStock/Archive Photos/Getty Images.

Printed in the United States of America

CONTENTS

Slave Societies vs. Societies With Slaves

The popular image of American slavery is of massive plantations with hundreds of black men and women laboring in cotton fields under harsh conditions. While this was certainly the case in the nineteenth century, cotton was not a **cash crop** during the colonial period. The early colonists grew tobacco, **indigo**, and rice, and used predominantly white English and Irish **indentured servants** as their labor force. It took several decades before African slavery and the **plantation system** took hold in the colonies.

During the late seventeenth and early eighteenth centuries, the plantation system came to dominate the agricultural economies of the Chesapeake and Low Country colonies. Labor-intensive cash crops increased the demand for African slaves. Attempts to profit using European indentured servants and Native American captives had failed, so colonists turned to the slave trade.

These restored buildings on Boone Hall Plantation once housed slaves in South Carolina. The plantation was founded in 1681.

As the slave population grew, colonial authorities placed increasingly harsh, race-based restrictions and punishments on slaves so that they could maintain order and control. By stripping black slaves of rights and giving lower-class whites a higher status, the planters were able to keep their white servants happy and loyal while reaping the financial benefits of both black and white labor.

Slavery took a much different form in the early colonial period than it did in the nineteenth century. It was not practiced uniformly across the regions. Each had different labor needs dictated by its economy. The New England colonies—Massachusetts, Rhode Island, Connecticut, and New Hampshire—were **mercantile** colonies. They focused on shipping, fishing, and trade. This was also true of the Middle colonies: New York (established in 1626 as New

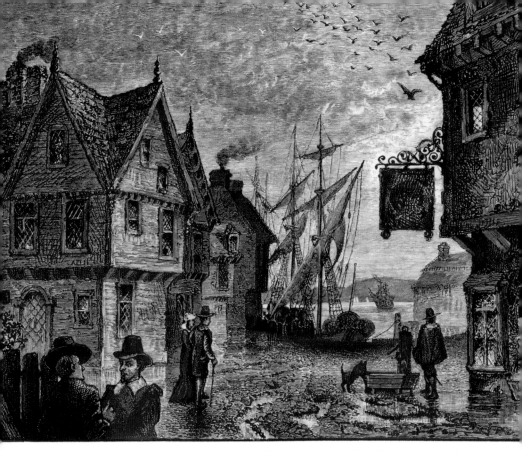

This nineteenth-century illustration depicts Boston in the 1660s. The economy of colonial Massachusetts was based on fishing, shipping, and trading.

Netherland by the Dutch), Delaware, New Jersey, and Pennsylvania. These colonies tended to have more urban development and established the first major port cities on the Atlantic Coast. The Southern colonies were very different. They had fewer cities and ports and remained mostly rural societies with agriculture-based economies. The Chesapeake colonies, Virginia and Maryland, grew tobacco. The Southern or Low Country colonies, Carolina and Georgia, grew rice and indigo. (The Carolina colony split into North Carolina and South Carolina in 1712.)

Historian Ira Berlin defines the major distinction between regions as one between "slave societies" and "societies with slaves." Societies with slaves were those in which slavery existed but was not the dominant labor system. Instead, slave labor was just one of many competing systems that also included family labor, indentured servitude, and wage labor. Societies with slaves tended to have fewer slaves and looser restrictions on the slaves they did have. They also had a higher free black population, and it was more likely for a slave to have some legal rights (such as the ability to sue in court), to marry and start a family, to be able to make some of their own money working a side job, and ultimately to gain their freedom.

Slave societies were societies in which slavery, being the dominant form of labor, shaped every other aspect of society, including the economy, politics, labor relations, and social identity. The slaveholding **planter class** was at the top of the social, political, and economic hierarchy in these societies. The relationship between master and slave shaped all aspects of life. Slave societies had a much more rigid and race-based class system and a small free black population. Slaves in these regions were subject to harsh punishment, had no legal rights, and little chance of ever gaining freedom for themselves or their children.

In the early years of the colonies, all were societies with slaves. But over time, the Southern colonies transformed into slave societies. The New England colonies did not make this transition, but slave labor was still crucial to their economic growth.

Philadelphia--Printed by E. Story, opposite I. Queen.

◇◇◇◇◇◇◇◇◇◇◇◇◇◇◇◇◇◇◇◇◇◇◇◇◇◇◇◇◇◇◇◇◇

This Indenture

WITNESSETH, That *Negro Shedrach, (born 9th January 1778)* *In Consideration of forty two Pounds ten Shillings paid by James Morris Esquire for Samuel Derrickson for the Manumission of the said Shedrach from Slavery.* *In Compliance with the Terms & Conditions of his said Manumission* hath put himself and by these Presents *with the advice and consent of his said late Master and Friend Samuel Derrickson* ———— doth voluntarily and of his own free will and accord put himself APPRENTICE to the said *James Morris of Montgomery County in the State of Pennsylvania Esquire* to learn the Art, Trade and Mistery, *and after the manner of an Apprentice to serve him the said James Morris his Executors administrators or Assigns* from the day of the date hereof, for and during, and to the full End and Term of *Eleven Years five Months & twenty five Days* next ensuing. During all which Term the said APPRENTICE his said Master Faithfully shall serve, his secrets keep his lawful commands every where readily obey-He shall do no damage to his said Master, nor see it to be done by others, without letting or giving notice thereof to his said Master.———HE shall not waste his said Master's goods, nor lend them unlawfully to any.———He shall not commit Fornication, nor contract Matrimony within the said term.———HE shall not play at Cards, Dice, or any other unlawful Game, whereby his said Master may have damage.———With his own goods nor the goods of others without licence from his said Master he shall neither Buy nor Sell.———HE shall not absent himself day nor night from his said Master's Service without his leave, nor haunt Ale Houses, Taverns, or Play Houses, but in all things behave himself as a Faithful apprentice ought to do during the said Term.———And the said MASTER shall use the utmost of his Endeavour to teach or cause to be taught or instructed the said Apprentice in the Trade or Mistery of *Husbandry or Farming* ———— and procure and provide for him sufficient Meat, Drink, *wearing Apparel* ———— Lodging and Washing fitting for an APPRENTICE during the said Term of *Eleven Years five Months and twenty five Days, and shall at the Expiration of the said Term give him two Suits of apparel one whereof to be new.*

AND For the true Performance of all and singular the Covenants and Agreements aforesaid, the said Parties bind themselves each unto the other, firmly by these Presents.———IN WITNESS whereof the said Parties have interchangeably set their Hands and Seals hereunto.———Dated the *Fifteenth* Day of *July* ———— Annoque Domini, One Thousand Seven Hundred and Ninety *Four*

Sealed and delivered in the presence of   *James Morris*

Samuel Derrickson

Hilary Baker, one of the

Aldermen of Philadelphia

From Servitude to Slavery

T he intent of the initial colonization efforts in British North America was not to import Africans for slave labor. White indentured servants were the most common laborers in the early decades of the colonies. However, as the colonies grew and the need for labor increased, settlers got involved in the transatlantic slave trade that brought millions of enslaved Africans to America. While the number of slaves in colonial America was quite small compared to the pre-Civil War period that followed, it was during the colonial period that the race-based slave system became an integral part of the nation's growing economy and was codified in colonial laws.

Indentured Servitude

In the 1610s, Jamestown colonist John Rolfe began experimenting with tobacco planting in Virginia. He

This Certificate of Indenture contracts a sixteen-year-old named Shadrach to James Morris of Philadelphia in 1794.

imported seeds from the West Indies, which produced a strain that was preferable to European tastes. Soon, there was a great market for it in England, and the tobacco boom of the 1620s solidified tobacco as the staple of Virginia's economy. The region's climate, soil, and proximity to waterways were conducive to growing and transporting tobacco, which could be produced with less land and fewer laborers than sugar on plantations in the West Indies.

Growing tobacco required year-round work and a lot of able-bodied people—many more than the early population of the colonies could supply. During the early colonial period, English indentured servants (mostly young men) were the preferred workers for tobacco production in the colonies. An indentured servant was a person who was contracted to work for a master in the colonies for a set number of years (usually four to seven) in exchange for their passage to the New World (which only the wealthy could afford), as well as their food, clothing, and shelter during the period of their service. After their contract was complete, they would receive **freedom dues,** which generally included a parcel of land and some supplies to help them get started. There were incentives for the wealthy landholders in the colonies to hire indentured servants: they acquired a workforce to expand the colonial economy, and they were granted additional land for each servant they contracted under the **headright system.**

The system began in Jamestown in 1618 as a way to increase the colonial population and the labor force. It granted 50 acres (20.2 hectares) of land to new settlers, and the land grant also applied to planters who contracted indentured servants. Since most young men in England could not afford their own passage, planters greatly increased their landholdings and personal wealth by bringing indentured servants to the colonies. This also made it relatively hard for any small, independent farmers to thrive in the region. The colony was mostly made up of large plantation holdings,

This painting by Sydney King depicts white farmers harvesting tobacco on a Virginia plantation, circa 1612.

which were spread out and isolated from one another, and there was little to no urban development. The population growth rate was slow in the early years of the Chesapeake colonies. There were very few female colonists, and there was a high mortality rate due to diseases such as malaria, dysentery, and typhoid fever.

It took only a few decades before it became more economically viable to use African slaves instead of white indentured servants. By the eighteenth century, the number of available European indentured servants dwindled, and those who were willing to accept contracts were more expensive. Potential servants were aware of the conditions for workers in the New World by this time, and many no longer believed that they would live a better life in the colonies. Colonists in the Chesapeake and elsewhere began to import African slaves to supplement their labor force.

African Servitude

The earliest Africans in the colonies were people from African port cities involved in trade with Europeans, especially the Dutch and Portuguese. They were known as "Atlantic Creoles" and were already familiar with European languages and customs. These people often spoke multiple languages and practiced a form of religion that blended Christianity with their traditional African beliefs and, in some cases, Islam. They had experience working alongside white European sailors and traders and sometimes served as interpreters. As the earliest laborers in the colonies, where the system of lifelong, hereditary slavery had not yet been established, Atlantic Creoles were able to better communicate and negotiate with European masters. They were more likely to be able to purchase their freedom, get married, and own property (including their own slaves).

The first documented Africans came to Jamestown as bound laborers in August of 1619. Colonist John Rolfe wrote:

> About the last of August came in a Dutch man of warre [ship] that sold us twenty [black slaves] … the Governor and Cape Marchant bought [them in exchange for food] at the easiest rates they could.

This account of the arrival of these men was long considered to be true; however, recent scholarship has uncovered that these twenty African men actually arrived on the English warship *White Lion*. Its crew had pirated the captives from a Portuguese slave ship on its way to Mexico. Rolfe's report was purposefully inaccurate to protect the English from Dutch claims of piracy.

The race-based system of lifelong, hereditary slavery did not exist in the early years of the colonies. The Africans who came to work in early colonial America were closer to indentured servants and worked alongside servants from the English working class. Black and white servants were treated mostly the same, lived in the same conditions, and were given the same freedoms after their term of service was completed. But both groups were subordinate to the wealthy, land-owning class.

Jamestown colonist John Rolfe experiments with early tobacco cultivation. Rolfe introduced tobacco to the colonies in the 1610s.

By the 1630s, there were already signs that the colonies were moving from indentured servitude toward a race-based system of slavery. Legal documents such as wills, deeds of sale, and inventory lists show that it was common for so-called "Negroes" to be held in lifetime service. One example is the will of a man named John Stoughton from Massachusetts. It lists two men alongside other possessions he owned when he died:

1 Stone horse, 1 Gelding Lame & Sickly

one man Negro named John & one Negro boy
named Peter

One beam Scales & 882 of Leaden weights

Three bbs flower, 2 firkins of butter, bad

These two men were given the same status in Stoughton's list of possessions as his lame horse.

Similar records also show that some black servants were set free after their contracted terms and went on to own their own property. One such man is Anthony Johnson, who arrived in Virginia in 1621. After his term of service at a tobacco plantation, where he met and married his wife Mary and had four children, he was given his freedom dues. The Johnsons purchased their own piece of land on the eastern shore of Virginia in 1640. By the following decade, they had more than 250 acres (101.2 ha) of land and five indentured servants of their own. In 1653, one of Johnson's black servants, John Casor, sued Johnson, claiming that he was still being held after his term of service had been completed. By this time, laws regarding lifetime servitude had been established in the colonies and in *Johnson v. Parker* (1655), the Northampton County court in Virginia found that Casor was to return to his master, Johnson, as his slave for life.

Early Colonial Slave Codes

The first evidence of legal, lifelong slave status in the colonies came in a legal case involving John Punch, an African servant who ran away along with two white servants. In 1640, the Virginia courts sentenced Punch to serve his master for "the time of his natural Life here or elsewhere." The white men only got extended terms of service. All three men were whipped.

Massachusetts was the first colony to officially legalize slavery when it passed the Body of Liberties in 1641. Part 91 of this document states:

This "marke" is part of Anthony Johnson's signature on a 1666 lease agreement for 300 acres (121 hectares) in Maryland with Stephen Horsey, a white man.

> There shall never be any bond slaverie, villinage
> or Captivitie amongst us unles it be lawfull
> Captives taken in just warres, and such strangers
> as willingly selle themselves or are sold to us.

Other colonies followed Massachusetts in establishing slave codes, with the most aggressive laws passed in the 1660s once slavery became more established in the Southern colonies.

Origins of the Transatlantic Slave Trade

The slave trade was thriving long before the British established their first colonies and began trafficking in human cargo. In the 1440s, the Portuguese established a trade route to West Africa. From the very beginning of the trade, Christianity was used to rationalize enslaving Africans, who were considered pagans in need of the civilizing effects of the Christian religion.

The Portuguese colonists in Brazil and the Spanish colonists in the West Indies imported African slaves from West and Central Africa to work on their sugar plantations. There was a high mortality rate and low birth rate among slaves, so the slave trade grew as the Portuguese and Spanish continually imported slaves to replace those who had died.

The Europeans purchased slaves from African rulers, who sold war captives from competing tribes and ethnic groups in exchange for European goods including textiles, rum, tobacco, weapons, and iron. Slavery in Africa was not race-based, as it would become in the Americas. African peoples identified with their specific tribe or village, not in terms of generalized identities such as "African" or "black."

This illustration depicts two jailers in Williamsburg, Virginia, standing around the stocks and pillory, which were used for the public punishment of slaves.

One of the most significant and racially charged was a 1662 Virginia law that stated:

> Whereas some doubts have arisen whether children got by an Englishman upon a negro woman should be slave or free, be it enacted and declared by this present grand assembly, that all children borne in this country shall be held bond or free only according to the condition of the mother, And that if any Christian shall commit fornication with a negro man or woman, he or she so offending shall pay double the fines imposed by the former act.

This law declared unequivocally that black slave women's children would be slaves. This made slavery hereditary, regardless of the status of the child's father (often the woman's white master). It also addressed the issue of **miscegenation** (interracial relationships) and made it illegal for "Christians" (i.e. white people) to have sexual relationships with black people.

In 1664, Maryland declared lifelong servitude for all black slaves. Later, New York, New Jersey, the Carolinas, and Virginia passed similar laws. That same year, Maryland passed a statute denying freedom to slaves who converted to Christianity. Virginia passed a similar measure in 1667. Colonial Christians believed that a fellow Christian could not be held in bondage, so the laws forbidding slave conversions ensured that slaves would not be able to use religion to gain their freedom, as some people had done in the earlier years of the colonies.

In 1669, Virginia passed a law—"An act about the casual killing of slaves"—stating that it is not a felony crime for a master to kill his slave because the slave is his property. This law stripped black slaves of their humanity and gave them the same status as livestock or land holdings; they were part of the estate of their master for life, as were any of their offspring, and they had no individual rights or freedoms.

As the colonies entered the eighteenth century, the rights of black slaves were even more severely restricted. The Virginia Slave Codes of 1705 became the standard followed by the other colonies. The document stated, in part:

> All servants imported and brought into the Country … who were not Christians in their native Country … shall be accounted and be slaves. All Negro, mulatto and Indian slaves within this dominion … shall be held to be real estate. If any slave resist his master, owner, or other person … correcting such slave, and shall happen to be killed in such correction it shall not be counted felony … the master, owner, or other person so giving correction shall be free of all punishment … as if such accident never happened.

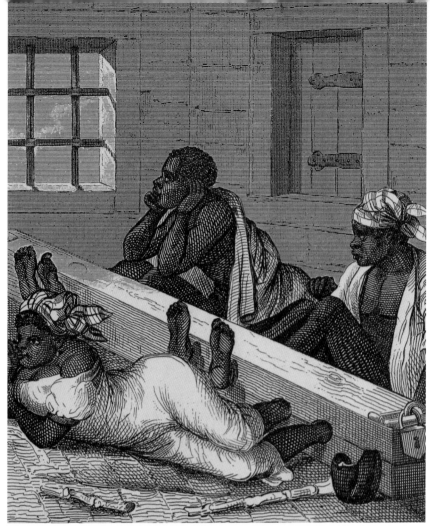

This engraving shows a group of black slaves in Brazil enduring punishment in the stocks. Brazil traded in slaves long before Colonial Americans did.

The code, which was explicitly race-based, also imposed gruesome physical punishments for non-violent offenses. A slave accused of theft would receive a whipping (sixty lashes), be put in the **stocks** (a wooden frame with holes in which the feet and hands can be locked), and have their ears cut off. For something as innocent as associating with white people, a slave could be whipped, maimed, or branded. For violent crimes such as rape or murder, a slave would be hanged.

Regional Differences in Slavery

T he experience of African slaves uprooted and brought to the New World was emotionally and physically traumatic. With no common language, religion, or kinship ties, it was an incredibly isolating experience. This was made even worse by the fact that slaves could always be sold away from the people they had come to know as family (blood or otherwise) at the whim of their master. Despite all this adversity, the enslaved Africans brought to the colonies and their descendants must be credited with much of the work of colony building.

The Middle Passage

The African people's passage to the Americas was often lethal before they could even reach the ship. Captives taken from the interior were marched hundreds of miles to the major ports on the West African coast and kept in the dungeons of fortified buildings known as slave castles. They could be held there for months until a slave ship was ready to depart for the Caribbean. The slavers would usually wait until they could completely fill the ship before making the long journey. The dungeons were overcrowded and revolts were common, always ending in violent suppression. Many died in the dungeons.

In his 1789 autobiography, former slave Olaudah Equiano (also known as Gustavus Vassa, the name given to him by his British master) recalls the horror he felt boarding a slave ship before his journey from West Africa to the British colony of Barbados:

> I now saw myself deprived of all chance of returning to my native country … I even wished for my former slavery in preference to my present situation, which was filled with horrors of every kind, still heightened by my ignorance of what I was to undergo … I was soon put down under the decks, and there I received such a salutation in my nostrils as I had never experienced in my life: so that, with the loathsomeness of the stench, and crying together, I became so sick and low that I was not able to eat, nor had I the least desire to taste any thing. I now wished for the last friend, death, to relieve me.

The sea voyage took several months and, before the crossing began, could also include stops at several ports along the West and Central African coast (stretching from present-day Senegal in the north to Angola in the south). Male slaves spent most of their time in the dark, poorly ventilated hull of the ship, naked and **shackled** together to prevent mutiny. Men were crammed in as tight as the slavers could get them, often unable to stand up or turn over. Since the slaves greatly outnumbered the crew, the crew used iron muzzles and whippings (or the fear of such things) to keep the slaves under their control. Women and young children were kept separate and given a bit more freedom of movement but were subject to violence and sexual abuse from the crewmen.

Many captives died due to illness caused by the unsanitary conditions and malnutrition. It was common for sick people to be thrown overboard and drowned at sea to avoid an epidemic of contagious disease on the ship. The severe physical and psychological trauma suffered aboard these ships caused many people to commit suicide at sea. Although the people aboard were from many different regions, spoke many different languages, and held diverse religious beliefs, it was a common belief among West African religions that the spirit returns home to one's ancestors in the afterlife. For many, suicide was preferable to life as a slave.

When Africans arrived at their destination—most often the West Indies but later at ports in the colonies—they were cleaned and prepared for public sale. They were stripped naked and subjected to intrusive examinations by prospective buyers. Those who were sold were in most cases separated from any family or kin groups they arrived with. Those who were not sold were left to die. Newly bought slaves, especially those arriving at Southern plantations, would be branded if they hadn't been already.

The Varieties of Slave Labor

There were two systems of labor on plantations: the **task system** and the **gang system**. Under the task system, slaves were assigned several specific tasks to complete in a day. The task system was used on rice plantations, in the naval stores industry (forest products such as pitch, turpentine, and tar), and in skilled labor positions. This was the easier of the two systems because there was less direct supervision, and it left slaves with more free time. Many slaves under the task system were expected to grow much of their own food in their spare time. Some slaves were allowed to sell any surplus crops they

This painting depicts a slave ship carrying African people. The men are packed in tightly and chained together to maximize profit and security for the slavers.

harvested, either to their owners or at public markets. The gang system was far more brutal. Slaves would work in large groups, under the supervision of white overseers or black drivers (foremen) who set the pace of work using whippings and other punishments. Work was from morning until night, with breaks only for meals, and left slaves with little time to themselves. The gang system was used on tobacco and sugar plantations.

By the middle of the eighteenth century, large plantations had become self-contained and self-sustaining, with slaves handling both skilled labor and manual labor. Skilled slaves were expected to handle a wide range of tasks and would serve variously as carpenters, **coopers**, boat builders, barn builders, **tanners**, cooks, blacksmiths, and tailors, among other things. The colonies were not yet developed enough for easy access to artisanal goods, so slaves were used to produce them at no additional cost to their master. South Carolina planter James Grant wrote in 1768, "In established plantations, the Planter has Tradesmen of all kinds in his Gang of Slaves, and 'tis a Rule with them, never to pay

KNOW all Men by these Presents,

That I *Isabella Kearney*

For and in Consideration of the Sum of *Six Pence*

Current Money of the Province of *New York* to me in Hand

paid, at and before the Ensealing and Delivery of these Presents, by

Negro Adam the Receipt whereof I do hereby acknowledge, and myself to be therewith fully satisfied, contented and paid: Have granted, bargained, sold, released; and by these Presents do fully, clearly and absolutely grant, bargain, sell and release unto the

Said Negro Adam his daughter Jenny

To have and to hold the said *Jenny*

unto the said *Negro Adam his* ——— Executors,

Administrators and Assigns, for ever. And I the said *Isabella Kearney* for myself, my Heirs, Executors and Administrators, do covenant and agree to and with the above named *Negro Adam his* ——— Executors, Administrators and Assigns,

to warrant and defend the Sale of the above-named *Jenny*

——————————— against all Persons whatsoever. In Witness

whereof, I have hereunto set my Hand and Seal, this *Nineteenth*

Day of *October* Annoq, Dom. One Thousand Seven Hund and *28*

Signed, Sealed and Delivered, in the Presence of

Isabella Kea

Sarah Skinner
Lambert Barberie

A 1718 bill of sale allowing a black man named Adam to buy the freedom of his daughter, Jenny, for sixpence from her master, Isabella Kearney of New York.

Money for what can be made upon their Estates, not a Lock, a Hinge, or a Nail if they can avoid it." Skilled slaves often got better treatment because they were more valuable and harder to obtain than a manual laborer who could be easily replaced.

Two provisions in the Navigation Acts, passed by Parliament between 1651 and 1673, increased the need for slave labor, especially in the South. The stipulation that the colonies could trade tobacco only with Britain reduced competition and lowered the price that landowners could get for their produce. This meant they had to produce tobacco more cheaply to earn a living. To do that required free labor. Also, the colonies could not manufacture any goods on a large scale that were being made in Britain. Landowners had to buy them from Britain or make those things themselves. This limited the ways colonists could make a living and contributed to the growth of the plantation economy.

The Chesapeake

The Chesapeake colonies used a comparatively small labor force initially made up of indentured servants, wage laborers, and slaves. The slaves who came to the Chesapeake at this time were Atlantic Creoles familiar with European languages and customs. The region had a white majority population and black and white servants worked together, lived in the same conditions, and even socialized with one another. Some (but not all) masters allowed slaves some financial independence and the freedom to marry and start a family, and they were more likely to manumit (set free) slaves or allow them to purchase their freedom. There were also small free black communities in the region.

In the late seventeenth century, the Chesapeake shifted to a plantation economy. There was a higher demand for slaves, who were now being imported from the African interior. Unlike the earlier Atlantic Creoles, these new arrivals were unfamiliar with Europeans. They came from all different parts of Africa and did not have shared linguistic, cultural, or religious ties. This prevented slaves in the region from forming large African American communities or extended kinship groups like those found in the Low Country region of South Carolina.

The white majority population allowed slaveholders more control over the daily lives of their slaves, with whom

Black slaves work on a tobacco plantation under the gang system, which was characterized by long hours under close supervision by white overseers.

they were in close proximity and constant contact. Labor conditions got much harsher, and slaveholders employed various methods of "breaking" their slaves. They were given meager clothing and food rations and had limited personal freedoms and mobility. They were also stripped of their history and cultural identity, including their names. African spiritual practices, languages, clothing, and traditional song, dance, and drumming were all outlawed in an attempt to break in slaves and keep them from forming a strong, unified community. Violence, or the fear of violent punishment, was the preferred method of controlling the increasing number of black slaves in the Chesapeake. The establishment of strict slave codes legalized race-based slave systems, ensuring the superiority of white masters and allowing complete control over the lives of their slaves.

South Carolina

South Carolina was founded in 1663 as the Province of Carolina. It included the territory that would become the colony of North Carolina in 1712. Many of Carolina's first settlers were Englishmen who came from Barbados with their slaves. These people were familiar with the success plantation owners in Barbados had using African slaves, and the colonists later used it as a blueprint when developing their own plantation system. The seaport of Charles Town (later Charleston) was established in 1670 and became North America's hub of the transatlantic slave trade.

In the early decades of the colony, indigo was the primary cash crop because planters did not know how to cultivate rice. They also exported Native American slaves to the West Indies and produced naval stores. It wasn't until the eighteenth century that South Carolina planters began to grow rice commercially with the help of the West African slaves from the "grain coast," who were familiar with the crop. They brought techniques such as the "heel-to-toe" method of planting and the use of woven **fanner baskets** to separate the grain from the husks. Soon, rice became the main export of South Carolina and grain-coast slaves were in high demand.

There was a high mortality rate among slaves in colonial South Carolina. Treatment of slaves by masters in this region could be especially brutal and negligent because they had no real economic incentive to keep their slaves alive. Because wealthy planters had easy access to the slave port of Charleston, they could easily purchase new Africans to replace those who had died. In the later years of the colony, the survival rate increased, and South Carolina had a black majority population. There were large African slave communities, which served kinship networks and preserved African culture and traditions. These slaves are the ancestors of today's Gullah peoples, a population of black Americans inhabiting the Sea Islands and the coastal regions of South Carolina, Georgia, and northeastern Florida. Their distinct culture and language evolved as a result of these large African slave communities in rice country, which were rural and isolated, and cut off from European influence.

Georgia

The Georgia colony was established in 1733 to serve as a military buffer between British Carolina and Spanish Florida. The founders of the colony wanted to ban slavery, but not because they were morally opposed to it. They envisioned the settlement as a place for small, independent farmers made up of England's poor, working-class families. The settlers would also serve as a military force to protect South Carolina from invasion and to stop runaway slaves from reaching freedom in Florida. By banning slave labor, they would be able to maintain a white majority population as well as avoid the class distinctions among whites in plantation societies where a small group of white plantation elites had most of the wealth.

The ban did not last, because colonists realized that the plantation slave labor system was much more lucrative. Colonists petitioned the Georgia trustees to overturn the ban. Slavery was legalized in Georgia in 1751 and grew rapidly, as South Carolina rice planters expanded into Georgia to increase their land holdings.

The city of Savannah served as a major port for the Atlantic slave trade from 1750, when the Georgia colony repealed its ban on slavery, until 1798, when the state outlawed the importation of slaves. Between 1750 and 1775, Georgia's slave population grew from less than five hundred to nearly eighteen thousand people.

New England

Slavery never took hold in New England to the extent that it did elsewhere in the colonies. The climate and soil of the region—which was similar to that of England—was not conducive to cash-cropping. It was far better suited to

Phillis Wheatley

Phillis Wheatley was the first African American woman to become a published poet. She was born in West Africa and sold into slavery when she was seven or eight years old. In 1761, she was brought to North America and purchased by John Wheatley of Boston, Massachusetts, to be a servant for his wife, Susanna. The Wheatleys and their children recognized Phillis's intelligence right away and the family taught her to read and write—something uncommon for slaves, especially females.

Wheatley started writing poetry at age thirteen. In 1773, her *Poems on Various Subjects, Religious and Moral* was published in London. The volume contains **elegies** and Christian-themed poems, as well as poems dealing with race and slavery. In this excerpt from "To the Right Honourable William, Earl of Dartmouth," she writes about being taken as a child:

I, young in life, by seeming cruel fate

Was snatch'd from Afric's fancy'd happy seat:

What pangs excruciating must molest,

What sorrows labour in my parent's breast?

Steel'd was that soul and by no misery mov'd

That from a father seiz'd his babe belov'd:

Such, such my case. And can I then but pray

Others may never feel tyrannic sway?

industries such as shipbuilding, fishing, whaling, and small-scale manufacturing. New England had small or family farms where colonists grew crops and raised livestock for sustenance, but the region did not have an **agrarian** economy.

Even though New England did not have a large slave population, the region benefited economically from slavery and the slave trade. Slaves were also crucial to the early years of the shipbuilding industry. They were often the ones who notched the trees and caught the sap required to make turpentine and tar. Beginning around the mid-1600s, American-made ships were actively involved in the slave trade transporting Native Americans in exchange for African slaves. Merchants engaged in trade with the West Indies, where all available land was used to grow cash crops (primarily sugar). Island planters had to import food, lumber, and other goods. The food being grown in New England supported the plantation system in the island colonies of Barbados and (later) Jamaica. Because West Indian planters would feed their slaves food that had gone bad, New Englanders could profit off of product, such as rotten fish, that they couldn't sell locally.

New Englanders who owned slaves usually owned four or fewer (with the exception of larger farms in Connecticut and Rhode Island, which could employ up to sixty slaves). Slaves in New England were primarily domestic laborers. However, domestic work included things like clearing forests for settlement, tilling the land, raising livestock, and planting crops. Men also worked as coach drivers, butlers, valets, or skilled laborers who learned a trade from their masters. Common trades included shipbuilding, carpentry, blacksmithing, tanning, and coopering. Slave women worked in the house doing the cooking, cleaning, laundry, making and repairing clothes, and nursing white children. These household tasks were quite labor-intensive in the colonial period. In addition, slave women were valued as tools for reproduction because any children they had would automatically be slaves.

CHAPTER THREE

Resistance and Rebellion

T he abolitionist movement had its beginnings in colonial America. The Quakers in Pennsylvania were the earliest voices to speak out against slavery. African American slaves did not participate in an organized movement as they would in the years leading up to the Civil War; however, slaves found small ways to resist in their everyday lives. Larger-scale resistance in the form of slave rebellions did occur, and while there were not very many, the few that did occur frightened the slaveholders, who passed even more restrictive laws to prevent insurrections.

The New York City Rebellions

The first large-scale, organized slave revolt in the colonies occurred in New York City in 1712. On the night of April 6, a group of slaves set fire to an outhouse belonging to one of their masters, Peter Van Tilburgh. This fire was meant as a signal to a larger group of slaves to begin the insurrection.

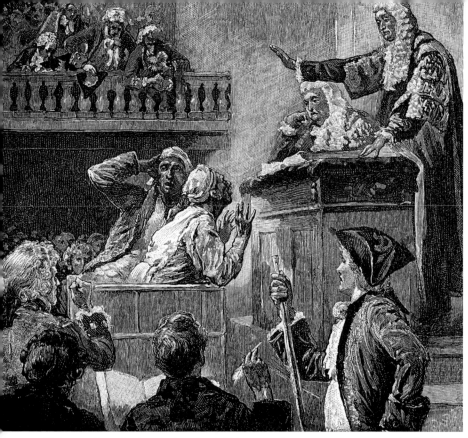

This woodcut depicts Judge Daniel Horsmanden sentencing accused rebel slaves Prince and Caesar to death in 1741.

As white neighbors came out of their homes to help put out the fire, they were attacked by armed slaves. New York governor Robert Hunter sent the militia after the rebel slaves, and many were captured. By the end of the night, nine white people were killed, and six more were injured. Six of the rebel slaves chose to commit suicide rather than be captured. Of the approximately forty slaves brought to trial, eighteen were acquitted and a few pardoned. The rest were cruelly executed in various ways including hanging, being burned alive, starvation, and being crushed by a wheel.

In response to the rebellion, the New York Assembly passed An Act for Preventing, Suppressing and Punishing the Conspiracy and Insurrection of Negroes and Other Slaves. This law gave masters the legal right to punish their slaves as harshly as they wanted, though "not extending to life or member." It also prohibited slaves from owning firearms, restricted their ability to congregate (no more than three slaves at a time), and discouraged **manumission** by requiring the master to pay a sum to both the government and the slave he wanted to set free.

Despite these restrictive laws, there was a second series of incidents in New York City. These events, also called the New York Conspiracy or the Great Negro Plot, occurred in the spring of 1741. There was a great deal of tension in New York at the time between black slaves and lower-class whites competing for work during an economic downturn. There are varying accounts of the events, but it is agreed that, on March 18, a fire broke out at Fort George, followed by a series of other fires in Lower Manhattan that may have been set by slaves. The fires continued over the course of the next few weeks, and white paranoia and rumors about a slave conspiracy took hold. On April 6, four fires broke out on the same day, and a witness claimed to have seen a black slave named Cuffee fleeing the scene of one of the fires.

Nearly two hundred people (both black slaves and lower-class whites) were arrested and tried by Judge Daniel Horsmanden. The main evidence in the trials was based on the unreliable testimony of sixteen-year-old Mary Burton, an Irish indentured servant who was pressured into testifying. Burton claimed that three slaves—named Cuffee, Caesar, and Prince—had collaborated with a group of lower-class whites and plotted to burn the city in exchange for their freedom. Despite the sketchy evidence, Horsmanden ordered the execution of nearly forty slaves, who were hanged or burned, as well as the hanging deaths of four white people. In addition, many more people—mostly black but some white—were exiled from the colony.

Horsmanden published his conclusions in 1744 in *A Journal of the Proceedings in the Detection of the Conspiracy*

Fort Mose was established on this spot in 1738 as a free black community and haven for runaway slaves in St. Augustine, Spanish Florida.

Formed by Some White People, in Conjunction with Negro and Other Slaves. He stated that the series of fires "were occasioned and set on Foot by some Villainous Confederacy of latent Enemies amongst us." Regarding Burton's testimony, Horsmanden wrote, "[Burton] was told, she must expect to be imprisoned in the Dungeon, if she continued obstinate; she then began to open, and named several Persons which she said she had seen … amongst the Conspirators, talking of the Conspiracy, who were engaged in it." Horsmanden's report of the trial makes it clear that Burton's testimony was dubious at best, and that she was pressured into naming names.

The Stono Rebellion

The largest slave rebellion in the British colonies occurred on September 9, 1739, near Charleston, South Carolina. The rebellion was led by a literate slave named Jemmy (also known as Cato). A group of twenty men gathered at the Stono River on a Sunday, a day and time when they knew their masters would be away from their plantations attending church

services. The rebels broke into a store, killing the owners and stealing weapons for their march south toward Spanish Florida. Florida had declared itself a safe haven for runaways in 1733, and by 1738, there was an established settlement of free runaway slaves called Fort Mose.

As the slaves marched, carrying banners that read "Liberty!," they recruited more runaways, burned plantations, and killed nearly thirty white people along the way. They crossed paths with a group of white men on horseback, including South Carolina's lieutenant governor William Bull, but the group fled to warn nearby slaveholders and gather a militia to put down the insurrection. The militia caught the slaves, now numbering almost eighty, at the Edisto River. Most of the slaves were killed on site or later captured and executed; those who weren't killed or executed were sold away to the West Indies.

The Stono Rebellion was the realization of the slaveholders' greatest fears. After it was put down, the colony enacted more restrictive laws and harsher punishments designed to

Arguments For and Against Slavery

The Quakers were the first group of white colonists to publicly object to slavery and the slave trade. Led by William Penn, the Quakers came to the colonies after being persecuted for their religious beliefs. The colony of Pennsylvania was established in 1681 and founded on a philosophy of religious tolerance and **pacifism**.

In 1688, four Quakers in the settlement of Germantown, Pennsylvania, issued a public antislavery statement. Their objection was based on the Bible's "Golden Rule": do unto others as you would have them do unto you. The Germantown Petition states, in part:

> ... we hear that the most part of such [slaves] are brought hither against their will and consent, and that many of them are stolen. Now, though they are black, we cannot conceive there is more liberty to have them slaves, as it is to have other white ones. There is a saying, that we should do to all men like as we will be done ourselves; making no difference of what generation, descent, or colour they are. And those who steal or rob men, and those who buy or purchase them, are they not all alike?

They found the institution of slavery—especially the separation of husbands and wives and the selling away of their children—to be morally wrong and contrary to Christian values. They believed that basic human rights should not be dependent on a person's race or ethnicity.

The Germantown Petition did not have any effect on the status of slavery in colonial Pennsylvania or elsewhere in the colonies. However, its significance lies in the idea of using the Bible as an argument against slavery.

Influential Puritan minister Cotton Mather of Massachusetts took an opposing view. Mather believed, as did most white colonists of the time, that there was nothing inherently unchristian about slavery. In 1696, he gave a sermon, "A Good Master Well Served," in which he stated:

> Give Ear, ye pitied Blacks, Give Ear! It is
> allowed in the Scriptures, to the Gentiles,
> That they May keep Slaves … You are better
> Fed & better Clothed & better Managed by
> far than you would be if you were your Own
> men … Though you are in Slavery to men,
> yet you shall be the Free-men of the Lord,
> the Children of God. Though you are Fed
> among the Dogs, with the [scraps] of our
> Tables, yet you shall at length Lie down unto
> a Feast with Abraham himself in the Heaven
> of the Blessed.

This **paternalistic** approach to slavery—that slaves were better off under the civilizing influence of white Christian masters—is a concept that was used well into the nineteenth century to justify slavery.

prevent future revolts and keep slaves in their place, raising up lower-class whites in the process. The Negro Act of 1740 prohibited slaves from growing their own food, assembling in large groups, learning to read, and earning their own money. In addition, there was a law passed requiring that there be at least one white person for every ten black people on a plantation so as to better monitor and control the slave population.

There is only one nonwhite account of the Stono Rebellion, that of George Cato, the great-great-grandson of the Stono Rebellion leader. His account, which was recorded in an interview by the Works Progress Administration in 1937, is based on his family's oral history of the event, passed down through the generations. Even though it is several generations removed from the event itself, the information Cato gives matches many other accounts and is significant as the only surviving account of events from a nonwhite perspective.

Cato told interviewers (who transcribed his dialect in a stereotypical way):

> I thinks de first Cato take a darin' chance on losin' his life, not so much for his own benefit as it was to help others. He was not [like] some slaves, much [a]bused by [their] masters. My kinfolks not [a]bused. [That is] why, I reckons, de captain of de slaves was picked by them. Cato was teached how to read and write by his rich master.

Cato goes on to say that his great-great-grandfather Cato spoke for the crowd as the militia approached:

> We don't [like] slavery. We start to [join the] Spanish in Florida. We surrender but we not whipped yet and we is not converted. [The] other forty-three men say: "Amen." They was taken, unarmed, and hanged by de militia. Long befo' dis uprisin', de Cato slave wrote passes for

slaves and do all he can to send them to freedom.
He die but he die for doin' de right, as he see it.

Individual Acts of Resistance

Organized slave revolts were the exception and not the rule
when it came to slave rebellion. That does not mean that
individual slaves did not fight back in small, subtle ways. There
were several common tactics that slaves used to rebel against
their masters. These included purposefully breaking tools,
faking illness, slowing down work through various forms of
sabotage, and even arson. Slaves also displayed statements of
individuality through their clothes, scarves, hairstyles, earrings,
and accessories they wore when they were not working in the
uniforms provided for them. Slave communities and families
reclaimed their history and culture through shared memories
and storytelling, keeping the oral history tradition alive. Slave
parents also gave their children African names, although
masters generally ignored them.

By far the most daring, and dangerous, act of individual
rebellion was escape. It was not uncommon for slaves to run
away from their masters—so much so that there were specific
laws regarding the return of runaways. During the colonial
era, slaves had fewer options than in later years when the
Northern states were free from slavery. Some fled to port
cities to try to get on a ship headed to Africa. Others fled to
areas with larger free black populations and tried to blend
in. Others headed south, seeking refuge in Spanish Florida,
especially in the 1730s. Some fled west to the frontier to live
with Native Americans. Others fled to swamps, mountains, or
dense forests some distance from their plantations and even
established settlements there. One such swamp settlement
existed north of the Savannah River in South Carolina
in 1765 and included approximately forty runaway slaves
(among them women and children).

CHAPTER FOUR

Slavery in the New Republic

B ritish attempts to control the growing colonies and consolidate their power caused them to pass restrictive laws, which led to colonial discontent and, ultimately, armed resistance. The colonists viewed British colonial rule as its own form of bondage, but the concepts of freedom and liberty for all, so crucial to the revolutionary ideology, stood in direct opposition to the institution of slavery.

Taxation Without Representation

The French and Indian War was an imperial conflict between the British and the French and was fought over control of the Ohio River Valley. This territory included the Mississippi River, which was a crucial trade route in the colonies. Territorial disputes between the French and the British, which started in 1754, resulted in Britain declaring war in

This engraving depicts colonists protesting the 1765 Stamp Act. The act taxed paper documents in the colonies and was passed by Parliament.

1756. The war ended in British victory in 1763, and the Treaty of Paris gave the British almost complete control of the colonies. They received Canada from France and Florida from Spain, and there was no longer any real threat or competition from foreign imperial powers.

Even though the British won the war, the military campaign in the colonies was expensive and left Britain with a large national debt. They believed that the American colonists (who benefitted from the British victory) should have to help pay the cost of the war as well as for the British troops stationed on the frontier. In 1765, Parliament passed the Stamp Act, a direct tax that applied to all paper documents in the colonies. This included wills, deeds, ship's papers, licenses, newspapers, pamphlets, and even playing cards and dice. The British government passed this act in Parliament without any representation or input from the colonial government, which caused dissent among the colonists, who felt that Britain was infringing on their freedoms. To the colonists, the British laws were reducing them to the status of slaves. There was an obvious hypocrisy to white colonists protesting their status as slaves to the British while also keeping black slaves, and many Americans began to question the institution of slavery. In order to rationalize the slave system on which much of their economy was based, Americans employed racist arguments about the natural inferiority of black people.

Racial Prejudice and Slavery

Thomas Jefferson's *Notes on the State of Virginia* (1785) is an excellent example of how race was used to justify the slave system. Jefferson was a slaveholder who supported gradual emancipation, but his beliefs about slavery were rooted in white supremacy. His support for abolition was contingent on the freed slaves being removed from Virginia. In *Notes*, he states his belief that black people are intellectually, creatively, and aesthetically inferior to white people. Jefferson wrote:

Comparing them by their faculties of memory, reason, and imagination, it appears to me that in memory [blacks] are equal to whites; in reason much inferior … in imagination they are dull, tasteless, and anomalous … never yet could I find that a black had uttered a thought above the level of plain narration; never see even an elementary trait of painting or sculpture. In music they are more generally gifted than the whites.

Jefferson draws the conclusion that black people are "inferior to the whites in the endowments both of body and mind." This type of pseudoscientific racial prejudice formed the foundation for colonists' assumptions that black people, by their very nature, were fit only for manual, unskilled labor. This included the belief their dark skin made them completely immune to the effects of heat and sun in the fields and therefore more suited to field labor than whites. In this way, white people became valued for their minds and black people for their bodies.

Independence For Some

The end of the French and Indian War marked the end of the colonial period, and the years that followed saw colonists making their own decisions, including developing their own independent system of government. The war and its aftermath had unified the colonies and a sense of national identity had developed. At the same time, tensions between Britain and the colonies were increasing as Britain, displeased with colonial resistance to authority, passed even more restrictive laws that the colonists actively rejected.

The Continental Congress was the first national governing body in what would soon become the United States of America, and in 1776, it issued the Declaration of Independence—the first of several documents that form the

A group of slaves greet their owner, Thomas Jefferson, upon his return to Monticello from Paris in 1789.

foundation of the United States government. The well-known preamble to the Declaration of Independence states:

> We hold these truths to be self-evident, that all men are created equal, that they are endowed, by their Creator, with certain unalienable Rights, that among these are Life, Liberty, and the pursuit of Happiness.

Thomas Jefferson, the delegate from Virginia, drafted the Declaration of Independence . He was one of many delegates—including George Washington, James Madison, and Benjamin Franklin—who owned slaves at the time this document, which declared liberty to be a fundamental human right granted by God, was created. Many colonists, including some of the delegates who owned slaves, struggled morally with slavery. Three of the best known were from Virginia. Jefferson himself called it a "hideous blot" on the nation. George Washington called it "repugnant." George Mason believed slavery was "evil." But in the debates that surrounded the establishment of the Constitution, the question of slavery was a political, not a moral one.

Constitutional Convention

The existence of slavery caused ideological problems for some of the delegates to the Constitutional Convention as they tried to develop a new government independent from the British. The Constitutional Convention was convened in Philadelphia in 1787 and was made up of fifty-five delegates from twelve states (all except Rhode Island). Its goal was to revise the 1781 Articles of Confederation drafted by the Second Continental Congress, which was the first federal constitution of the United States of America. The Articles of Confederation did not address slavery on a federal level, leaving regulation of the institution to the individual states.

Slavery was a major issue debated among the delegates drafting the United States Constitution. They were split along North-South lines. The delegates' goal was to form a strong central government and a union of all the states, but they disagreed on the organization of the legislative branch of government—specifically taxation and representation in Congress. States with large populations wanted representatives in both legislative houses to be based solely on population size, while smaller states wanted all states to have equal representation in both houses (as they had under the Articles of Confederation). They eventually reached

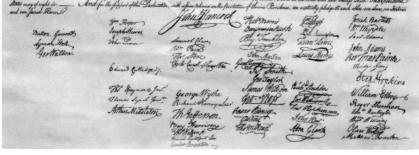

The Declaration of Independence stated that all men have rights "endowed by their Creator" but the right of liberty was not extended to slaves at that time.

a compromise in which the Senate would be equal (two representatives per state) and the House of Representatives would be population-based. In order to reach this "Great Compromise," the framers of the constitution were forced to confront the issue of slavery.

Debates were not about whether slavery was right or wrong but about whether slaves counted as people in calculating state populations. Population numbers determined both taxation and representation for the individual states in the federal government. The slave states in the South wanted the slave population to be included in the total count. At the time, slaves represented one-fifth of the population of the United States and were concentrated in the South. By counting slaves, the Southern states would increase their political power, both in the number of representatives they had in the House and in the number of electoral votes they had in presidential elections. It would also increase the amount of taxes they paid to the federal government, but since Southern states' wealth was based on slave labor, they were willing to accept higher taxes. Southern delegates would not accept any document that did not secure their right to hold slaves.

Debating the Slavery Question

From August 21 to 22, 1787, the delegates debated the slavery question. These debates were recorded in James Madison's "Notes on the Debates in the Federal Convention." During the August 21 session, Madison's notes recorded the debate over South Carolina's proposal to prohibit federal regulation of the Atlantic slave trade. Luther Martin (Maryland) was a slaveholder who believed that "it was inconsistent with the principles of the Revolution, and dishonorable to the American character, to have such a feature in the Constitution." John Rutledge (South Carolina) responded that:

> Religion and humanity had nothing to do with this question … The true question at present is, whether the Southern States shall or shall not be parties to the Union. If the Northern States consult their interest, they will not oppose the increase of slaves, which will increase the commodities of which they will become the carriers.

JOHN RUTLEDGE

Nat-1739 — Ob-1800

John Rutledge of South Carolina argued for slavery at the Constitutional Convention. He later served as a Chief Justice of the US Supreme Court.

Oliver Ellsworth of Connecticut believed that it should be left to the individual states to decide and that "what enriches a part enriches the whole, and the States are the best judges of their particular interest." Charles Pinckney of South Carolina responded that, "South Carolina can never receive the plan if it prohibits the slave-trade."

The debates continued on August 22. Connecticut delegate Roger Sherman disapproved of the slave trade but thought that things should be left as-is for the sake of the Union. He stated that "it was expedient to have as few objections as possible to the proposed scheme of government" and "observed that the abolition of slavery seemed to be going on in the United States, and that the good sense of the several States would probably by degrees complete it."

George Mason, who owned hundreds of slaves, believed strongly that the federal government should have the power to regulate slavery. Mason stated:

> Slavery discourages arts and manufactures. The poor despise labor when performed by slaves. They prevent the emigration of whites, who really enrich and strengthen a country … Every master of slaves is born a petty tyrant. They bring the judgment of Heaven on a country. As nations cannot be rewarded or punished in the next world, they must be in this. By an inevitable chain of causes and effects, Providence punishes national sins by national calamities.

Even though he was a slaveholder, Mason expressed antislavery beliefs, but these were based on the effect of the slave system on white Christians and the fate of the new nation, not out of any concern for the well-being of the slaves themselves.

Ellsworth, who had never owned slaves, reiterated his belief that the issue should be left to the states, adding that, "as population increases, poor laborers will be so plenty as to render slaves useless. Slavery in time, will not be a speck in our country." But South Carolina's General Charles Cotesworth Pinckney (not to be confused with the other Charles Pinckney from South Carolina) declared unequivocally that, "South Carolina and Georgia cannot do without slaves." General Pinckney contended that, "the importation of slaves would be for the interest of the whole Union. The more slaves, the more produce to employ the carrying trade; the more consumption also; and the more of this, the more revenue for the common treasury." Rutledge was equally insistent, stating that, "if the Convention thinks that North Carolina, South Carolina, and Georgia, will ever agree to the plan, unless their right to import slaves be untouched, the expectation is vain. The people of those States will never be such fools as to give up so important an interest."

The proslavery Southern delegates were immovable on the issue of slavery, but ultimately several compromises were reached, and the US Constitution was ratified on June 21, 1788.

What the Constitution Says About Slavery

The words "slave" and "slavery" were not used in the United States Constitution, but the document still managed to codify and strengthen the institution of slavery in the United States. Article 1, Section 2 of the Constitution included what became known as the Three-Fifths Compromise (first adopted by the Continental Congress). This clause states, in part, that representatives and taxation shall be determined according to population "which shall be determined by adding to the whole Number of free Persons, including those bound to Service for a Term of Years, and excluding Indians not taxed, three fifths of all other Persons." The terms "other persons" is used in lieu of the word "slaves."

Another section that directly addressed slavery is Article 1, Section 9, which stated that Congress could not abolish the Atlantic slave trade or ban importation of slaves until 1808—twenty years after the Constitution went into effect. Perhaps the most significant part of the Constitution with regard to slavery was the so-called Fugitive Slave Clause (Article 4, Section 2, Clause 3). This stated that, "No Person held to Service or Labour in one State, under the Laws thereof, escaping into another, shall, in Consequence of any Law or Regulation therein, be discharged from such Service or Labour,

This oil painting by Howard Chandler Christy, *Scene at the Signing of the Constitution of the United States*, depicts the events of September 17, 1787.

but shall be delivered up on Claim of the Party to whom such Service or Labour may be due." Again, without using the word "slave," the Constitution solidified the rights of slaveholders to recapture their slaves anywhere in the nation, including locations where slavery had been or would be abolished. This law also applied to indentured servants and apprentices.

The compromises regarding slavery that were included in the final version of the United States Constitution were not a permanent solution to the problem. With their rights to slave property constitutionally granted, the slave system in the South became more firmly entrenched in that region. As the United States expanded westward in the nineteenth century, the compromises that had kept a balance of power between the North and South started to break down. By the time the nation was on the verge of the Civil War, the slave system looked very different than it had during the colonial era, but it was during the early formative years of the colonies that race-based slavery was normalized and protected by the nation's highest laws.

Chronology

Dates in green pertain to events discussed in this volume.

April 10, 1606: King James I issues the First Virginia Charter to the Virginia Company, authorizing its leaders to establish the Virginia colony and beginning the Colonial period.

May 13, 1607: The first permanent English colony in the New World is established at Jamestown, Virginia.

July 30, 1619: The House of Burgesses, the first legislative assembly in the colonies, convenes.

August 1619: The first documented Africans arrive in Jamestown, Virginia.

September 6, 1620: The *Mayflower* leaves Plymouth, England, for North America.

November 9, 1620: The Pilgrims see land for the first time on their trip; it is Cape Cod.

November 11, 1620: Adult males on the *Mayflower* sign the Mayflower Compact.

December 21, 1620: The Pilgrims land in Plymouth, Massachusetts.

Fall 1621: The Pilgrims and the Wampanoag celebrate a fall harvest festival together in what is considered the first Thanksgiving celebration in America.

November 9, 1621: The *Fortune* arrives in Plymouth, carrying additional people but no supplies.

May 1624: The Dutch establish the colony of New Netherland.

March 4, 1629: The Massachusetts Bay Company receives a charter from Charles I to trade in New England; the company's Puritan leaders land at Salem on June 12, 1630.

1632: Charles I grants to Lord Baltimore territory north of the Potomac, which becomes Maryland; the king does not restrict residency to Protestants, so Catholics are allowed.

March 3, 1634: The *Ark* and the *Dove* sail up the Chesapeake Bay, carrying the first settlers of Maryland; on March 25, the group purchases land from the Natives and names their settlement St. Mary's.

June 1636: Roger Williams founds the colony of Rhode Island.

December 1638: The first American-built slave ship,

Desire, transports Pequot Indians to the West Indies in exchange for African slaves.

1641: Massachusetts becomes the first colony to legalize slavery with the Body of Liberties.

December 1662: A Virginia law states that the slave status of black children is based on the status of the mother, introducing the system of hereditary, race-based slavery to the colonies.

September 7, 1664: The Dutch surrender New Amsterdam to the English, who rename the colony New York.

September 1664: Maryland mandates lifelong servitude for all black slaves and passes a statute denying freedom to slaves who converted to Christianity. Other colonies adopt similar laws over the next few years.

1669: A Virginia law—"An act about the casual killing of slaves"—states that it is not a felony crime for a master to kill his slave because the slave is his property.

June 24, 1675: The Native population attacks Swansea, Massachusetts, at the start of an attempt to wipe out the English settlers with a massive military action. This starts King Philip's War.

August 12, 1676: King Philip's War ends.

September 19, 1676: Jamestown is burned during Bacon's Rebellion; the rebellion ends the next month following the death of its leader, Nathaniel Bacon.

March 4, 1681: Charles II grants William Penn a charter for what becomes Pennsylvania.

April 1688: The Germantown Petition written by Pennsylvania Quakers becomes the first public antislavery statement issued by a white organization.

May 1689: King William's War, the first French and Indian War, begins with the British declaring war on France; the war ends in 1697 with the Treaty of Ryswick.

October 7, 1691: The Province of Massachusetts Bay is chartered, merging the Massachusetts Bay Colony with the Maine and Plymouth territories to form a larger colony.

June 8, 1692: The Plymouth General Council has its last meeting.

May 4, 1702: Queen Anne's War, the second French and Indian War, begins; it ends in 1713 with France ceding Newfoundland and Nova Scotia to Britain.

February 29, 1704: French and Indian forces kill fifty residents and take more than one hundred captives in a raid on Deerfield, Massachusetts.

1705: The Virginia Slave Codes (which would become the model for the other colonial laws) further restrict the freedoms of slaves and expand the rights of slave owners.

September 22, 1711: The Tuscarora Indian War begins in North Carolina; surviving Native Americans move north to New York to join the League of Six Nations.

April 6, 1712: The first New York City slave rebellion occurs, leading New York to pass laws restricting the freedoms of slaves and prevent future rebellions.

April 21, 1732: King George signs a charter creating Georgia and establishes a board of trustees to govern the colony.

April 3, 1735: Britain ratifies an act banning slavery in Georgia.

September 9, 1739: Slaves in South Carolina begin the Stono Rebellion, which ends with between forty-two and forty-seven whites and forty-four blacks killed; it is the largest slave rebellion in the colonies.

April 21, 1741: A jury is impaneled to hear testimony on an alleged plot to burn New York City; this incident was termed the Great Negro Plot of 1741 and the New York Conspiracy of 1741.

January 1, 1751: A resolution passed by the state's House of Commons to allow slavery in Georgia takes effect.

May 28, 1754: Troops representing France and Great Britain and their Native Americans allies battle at Fort Duquesne in a struggle for control of the Ohio River Valley. This is the first fighting in what becomes the Seven Years' War, otherwise known and the French and Indian War.

May 15, 1756: Britain declares war on France, officially starting the French and Indian War.

September 13, 1759: British forces capture Quebec City in the climactic battle of the French and Indian War; the leaders of both armies, General Louis-Joseph de Montcalm of the French and Commander James Wolfe of the British, die in the fighting.

February 10, 1763: The signing of the Treaty of Paris ends the French and Indian War. This closes the Colonial period.

August 21–22, 1787: The delegates debate slavery at the Constitutional Convention.

Glossary

agrarian Relating to the land, especially the use of land for farming.

cash crop A crop (such as tobacco or cotton) that is grown to be sold rather than for use by the farmer.

cooper Someone who makes or repairs casks and barrels.

elegy A song or poem expressing sorrow or lamentation, especially for one who is dead.

fanner basket A coiled woven basket used for winnowing rice grains brought to North America by West African slaves.

freedom dues The sum of money, land, and/or supplies that a master owes an indentured servant after the person has completed a contracted term of service.

gang system A system of plantation slave labor in which slaves worked a full day in large groups supervised by white overseers or black drivers.

headright system A system in which each settler in the colonies would receive a parcel of land. The system also allowed colonists to receive land grants for each indentured servant they hired.

indentured servant A person who is contracted to work a certain number of years in exchange for passage to the colonies, shelter, food, and clothing, and freedom dues when their term of service is complete.

indigo A tropical plant of the pea family, which was formerly widely cultivated as a source of dark blue dye.

manumission The act of a master granting freedom to a slave.

mercantile The business of building national economic strength by exporting more goods than are imported. This meant regulating trade between homeland and its colonies to ensure a favorable balance of trade for the homeland.

miscegenation Mixing of races, including marriage, cohabitation, or sexual intercourse between a white person and a member of another race.

pacifism The belief that any violence, including war, is unjustifiable under any circumstances, and that all disputes should be settled by peaceful means.

paternalism The practice by authority figures of restricting the freedom of those subordinate to them in the supposed best interest of those being controlled.

plantation system A large-scale agricultural operation on which resident slaves were put to work producing cash crops for the financial gain of their owners.

planter class A powerful class consisting only of wealthy white men who owned large amounts of property and more than twenty slaves.

shackle A metal ring or fastening, usually part of a pair connected by a chain and used to secure a person's wrists and ankles.

stocks A wooden frame with holes in which the feet and hands can be locked.

tanner A person who is employed to tan animal hides into leather.

task system A system of plantation slave labor in which slaves were assigned several specific tasks to complete within a day's work.

Further Information

Books

Schneider, Dorothy, and Carl J. Schneider. *Slavery in America: From Colonial Times to the Civil War*. New York: Facts on File, 2000.

Taylor, Alan. *Colonial America: A Very Short Introduction*. New York: Oxford University Press, 2013.

Williams, Heather Andrea. *American Slavery: A Very Short Introduction*. New York: Oxford University Press, 2014.

Wood, Betty. *Slavery in Colonial America, 1619–1776*. Lanham, MD: Rowman & Littlefield, 2005.

Wood, Peter H. *Strange New Land: Africans in Colonial America*. New York: Oxford University Press, 2003.

Websites

Encyclopedia Virginia: Indian Enslavement in Virginia
https://www.encyclopediavirginia.org/Indian_Enslavement_in_Virginia
A history of the enslavement of Native Americans in Virginia, by both settlers and other Natives, during the Colonial period is told with photos, audio recordings, and stories.

Lowcountry Digital History Initiative
http://ldhi.library.cofc.edu/exhibits/show/africanpassageslowcountryadapt

An online exhibition series about the history of slavery, plantations, and the trans-Atlantic slave trade from the Atlantic World to Charleston and the South Carolina Lowcountry.

PBS: Slavery and the Making of America
http://www.pbs.org/wnet/slavery/index.html

A comprehensive history of slavery in early America, including historical essays, primary source documents, timelines, and multimedia resources.

Voyages: Transatlantic Slave Trade Database
http://slavevoyages.org

This resource has information on more than thirty-five thousand transatlantic slaving journeys, including historical essays on the slave trade as well as maps showing trade routes, a timeline, and a searchable database of voyages and African names.

Bibliography

Books

Berlin, Ira. *Many Thousands Gone: The First Two Centuries of Slavery in North America*. Cambridge, MA: Harvard University Press, 1998.

Equiano, Olaudah. *The Interesting Narrative of the Life of Olauduh Equiano, or Gustavas Vassa, The African*. CreateSpace Independent Publishing Platform, 2014, reissue of book published in 1789.

Horton, James Oliver, and Lois E. Horton. *Slavery and the Making of America*. Oxford, UK: Oxford University Press, 2006.

Morgan, Edmund S. *American Slavery, American Freedom: The Ordeal of Colonial Virginia*. New York: W.W. Norton & Co., 2003.

Morgan, Philip D. *Slave Counterpoint: Black Culture in the Eighteenth Century Chesapeake and Lowcountry*. Chapel Hill, NC: University of North Carolina Press, 1998.

Smith, Mark M. *Stono: Documenting and Interpreting a Southern Slave Revolt*. Columbia, SC: University of South Carolina Press, 2005.

Taylor, Alan. *Colonial America: A Very Short Introduction*. New York: Oxford University Press, 2013.

Warren, Wendy. *New England Bound: Slavery and Colonization in Early America*. New York: W.W. Norton & Co., 2016.

Williams, Heather Andrea. *American Slavery: A Very Short Introduction*. New York: Oxford University Press, 2014.

Wood, Betty. *Slavery in Colonial America, 1619–1776.*
Lanham, MD: Rowman & Littlefield, 2005.

———— *Slavery in Colonial Georgia, 1730–1775.* Athens, GA:
University of Georgia Press, 2007.

Wood, Peter H. *Black Majority: Negroes in Colonial South
Carolina from 1670 through the Stono Rebellion.* New York:
W.W. Norton & Co., 1975.

———— *Strange New Land: Africans in Colonial America.* New
York: Oxford University Press, 2003.

Wright, Donald R. *African Americans in the Colonial Era:
From African Origins through the American Revolution.*
Wheeling, IL: Harlan Davidson, 2010.

Online Articles

Cato, George. "A Family Account of the Stono Uprising,
ca. 1937." National Humanities Center. Accessed April
10, 2017. http://nationalhumanitiescenter.org/pds/
becomingamer/peoples/text4/stonorebellion.pdf

Horsmanden, Daniel. "A Journal of the Proceedings in the
Detection of the Conspiracy Formed by Some White
People, in Conjunction with Negro and Other Slaves." The
Gilder Lehman Institute of American History. Originally
published in 1744. Accessed April 10, 2017.
https://www.gilderlehrman.org/history-by-era/thirteen-
colonies/resources/new-york-conspiracy-1741

Madison, James. "Notes on the Debates in the Federal
Convention of 1787." The Avalon Project. Accessed April
10, 2017. http://avalon.law.yale.edu/subject_menus/
debcont.asp

"Mercantilism." Investopedia. Accessed April 26, 2017. http://
www.investopedia.com/terms/m/mercantilism.asp

"Resolutions of The Germantown Mennonites, February 18,
1688." The Avalon Project. Accessed April 10, 2017. http://
avalon.law.yale.edu/17th_century/men01.asp

"What About Slavery is Unchristian? American Protestant
Views, 1690–1760." National Humanities Center. Accessed
April 10, 2017. http://nationalhumanitiescenter.org/pds/
becomingamer/ideas/text3/slaveryunchristian.pdf

Wheatley, Phillis. "To the Right Honourable William, Earl of
Dartmouth." PBS.org. Accessed April 10, 2017. Originally
published 1773. Citation from *The Collected Works of Phillis
Weatley*, John Shields ed. New York: Oxford University
Press, 1988. http://www.pbs.org/wgbh/aia/part2/2h20t.
html

Index

Page numbers in **boldface** are illustrations. Entries in **boldface** are glossary terms.

About the Author

ALISON MORRETTA holds a Bachelor of Arts in English and Creative Writing from Kenyon College in Gambier, Ohio, where she studied literature and American history. She has written many nonfiction titles for middle and high school students on subjects such as American literature, the abolitionist movement, the civil rights era, and westward expansion. She lives in New York with her loving husband, Bart, and their rambunctious Corgi, Cassidy.